W9-BIL-032

less sticky than a Band-Aid

faster-acting than time-release capsules

Dr. Amelia's

Boredom Survival

Guide

no child-proof cap necessary

easier to swallow than chalky pills

better-tasting than that nasty cough syrup

GLOR GRU SYR

First Aid for Rainy Days, Boring Errands,

Waiting Rooms, Whatever!

by Marissa Moss

(and Dr. Amelia, brain surgeon)

thermometer

American Girl

IN CASE OF EMERGENCY

TURN PAGE

VACCINATE YOURSELF AGAINST BOREDOM 31¢

This guide is
dedicated, with great
excitement, to
Brion,
who practically never gets bored.

Copyright © 1999 by Marissa Moss

Are you bored enough to bother to read this? Then you really need this guide!

Pleasant Company
Publications
8400 Fairway Place
Middleton, Wisconsin 53562

Book Design by Amelia

Library of Congress Cataloging-in-Publication Data
Moss, Marissa

Dr. Amelia's boredom survival guide: first aid for rainy days, boring errands, waiting rooms, whatever! / by Marissa Moss
p. cm.
"American Girl."
Summary: While waiting for her sister's medical appointment, a bored Amelia creates a handwritten book of fifty suggestions for passing the time.
ISBN 1-56247-794-3 (pbk.)
I. American Girl (Middleton, Wis.)   II. Title.
PZ7.M8535 Dr 1999
[Fic] -- dc21   98-54758
                                                          CIP
                                                          AC

haven't you forgotten someone?

First Pleasant Company Publications printing, 1999

An Amelia™ Book
American Girl™ is a trademark of Pleasant Company.
Amelia™ and the black-and-white notebook pattern
are trademarks of Marissa Moss.

Manufactured in Singapore

Prevent Tedium-Foot 12¢

Is this part of a jump rope rhyme?

00 01 02 03 04 TWP 10 9 8 7 6 5 4 3

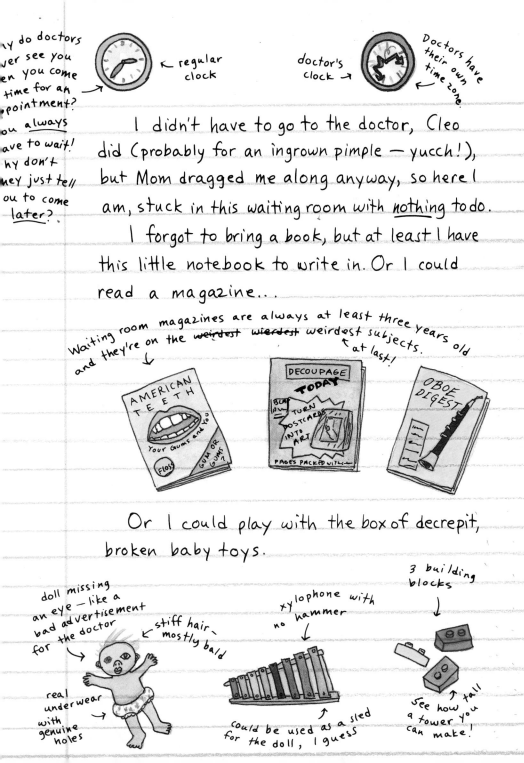

Why do doctors never see you when you come on time for an appointment? You always have to wait! Why don't they just tell you to come later?

← regular clock

doctor's clock →

Doctors have their own time zone.

I didn't have to go to the doctor, Cleo did (probably for an ingrown pimple — yucch!), but Mom dragged me along anyway, so here I am, stuck in this waiting room with <u>nothing</u> to do.

I forgot to bring a book, but at least I have this little notebook to write in. Or I could read a magazine...

Waiting room magazines are always at least three years old and they're on the weirdest weirdest weirdest subjects.
↑ at last!

AMERICAN TEETH
Your Gums and You
Floss
GUM OR GUMS?

DECOUPAGE TODAY
TURN POSTCARDS INTO ART
PAGES PACKED WITH—

OBOE DIGEST

Or I could play with the box of decrepit, broken baby toys.

doll missing an eye — like a bad advertisement for the doctor →

← stiff hair — mostly bald

real underwear with genuine holes →

xylophone with no hammer ↓

could be used as a sled for the doll, I guess

3 building blocks ↓

↑ tall
see how a tower you can make!

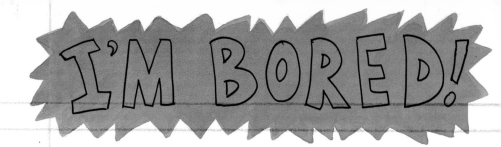

I'M BORED!

All right, I've had it! Since there's nothing here for me, I'll <u>make</u> something. I'll make a guide of 50 fun, cool things to do, so if I'm ever stuck in a boring place like this again, I'll have my handy-dandy guide to rely on.

Potential Boring Situations

MAKING FACES

Thing to Do #1
   See if you can touch the tip of your
nose with your tongue.

↑ use a mirror!

Thing to Do #2
   Try to wiggle your ears and eyebrows at
   the same time.

↑
fake eyebrows
don't count

Thing to Do #3
Practice winking.

This is as close as
I can get — I just
can't wink!

Time used up: A wink in time saves nine.

Try to look cross-eyed,
but not for too long or
your eyes will get stuck
that way
(says Mom).
↓

Look, Ma,
no hands!

she has the looooongest tongue I've
ever seen — she can lick ice cream
off her chin!

TONGUE TO-DO'S

Thing to Do #4

Now that your tongue is warmed up, make some tongue twisters and say them as fast as you can.

mmblgm

↳ tongue knot

Here's some I invented:

"Clunky Cleo crawled and clawed into claustrophobic caves."

piles of peach, prune, and pecan pie

perky, peppy pig pacers

"Pink pigs prance prettily past plenty of prune pie."

Carly has the fastest tongue in the West — no one says "She sells seashells down by the seashore" faster!

Time used up: However long it takes before your tongue gets numb.

NOISES PAGE

↑ oops! __not__ noses — __noises__!

Thing to Do #5

Try to make as many noises as you can without using your voice, like snapping your fingers, drumming them on the table, tapping your toes, popping your cheek with your finger. Are you driving people crazy yet? Then STOP IT!

WARNING: Make __these__ noises only when no one else is around or no one will __ever__ want to be around you.

Thing to Do #6 ↙

Enough annoying noises — now try to make gross noises. Burp as loud as you can, suck your teeth, smack your lips, snort.

nubby waiting room carpet ↓

knocked flat by a __powerful__ BURP! ↓

Time used up: Depends on how much grossness you can take.

drip drip

tip tap tip tap

clip clop clip clop

SOUND EFFECTS

Thing to Do #7
   Think up comic book sound effects for real life. (I mean, who uses **BIF!** and **WHAM!** ?)

I got this idea from Maya — she loves to read comic books.

when you blow a wrapper off a straw

THWIP

fwish!

SMOOF!

when you spit out toothpaste

when you plop down on an armchair or a sofa

Time used up: Holy fish sticks, Batman, it's time for **GAWOOMMMPKAA!**

EYE TRICKS

Thing to Do #8
   Stare hard at something — a lamp, a doorknob, a chair leg. Stare until you see two of whatever it is. Try to make the two things one again. Now two again. Now one.
   If you can't make yourself see double, see how long you can stare without blinking.

   Time used up: Until your eyes see triple.

Which lamp is the real one?

Made ya blink!

"i say, eyes are made to use, not to abuse!"
← the mom warning finger — beware!

Answer: None. These are all drawings of lamps. Gotcha!

JUST LOOKING, THANKS

Thing to Do #9

Make the cracks in the ceiling into pictures, like you do with clouds. Find a dragon, a cat, a secret message.

If the ceiling is made of that ugly speckled tile, skip this and rate the room down 2 points in Thing to Do #12

Thing to Do #10

If there's wallpaper, make a path on it with your eyes — create a wallpaper maze! But don't get lost or your eyes will be stuck looking at that wallpaper forever!

Leah likes to pretend she's a spy and has to memorize all the details in the room because something is a bomb in disguise.

Veeeery interesting!

magnifying glass

Help! I can't find my way!

Thing to Do #11

Balance pennies (or other coins) on the baseboard. See how many you can line up. If you want to get fancy and you have a lot of different coins, make a pattern or pretend the faces are talking to each other.

Long time no see, George.

I'm not George, I'm Jefferson.

No, I am!

What happened to Honest Abe?

Thing to Do #12

Rate the room you're in from 1 to 10, 1 being the ugliest, 10 the most beautiful.

Deduct 2 points if the rug is an unnameable color (like pinkish-brownish-yellowish).

Deduct 1 point for every picture that looks the same upside down as right-side up.

Time used up: Lemme out of this room — I've spent waaay too much time in here!

↖ oops! It's hung upside down!

← Paintings that look like a 2-year-old did them get a −10 score

Is it the picture belonged in a museum — deduct 5 points

Thing to Do #13
   Don't do anything at all! Thirteen is
an unlucky number, so just skip it!

Time used up: The time it took you
to read this page.

EEEEK! The curse
of 13 is spreading!
↘

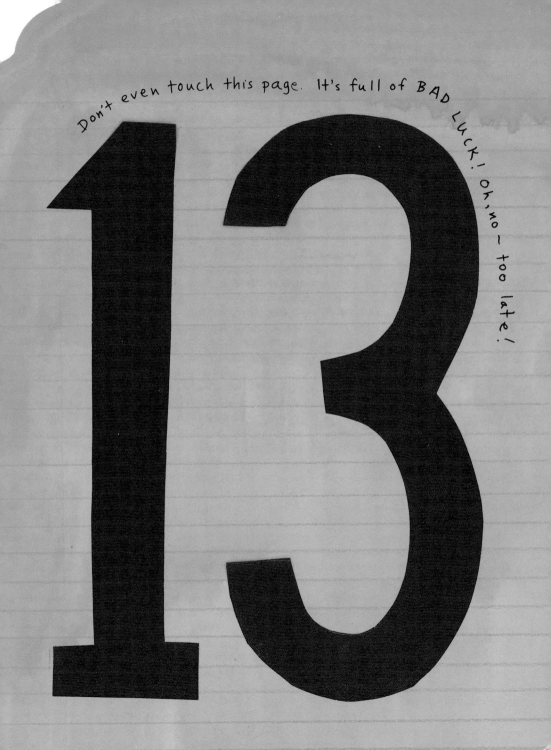

FORTUNE TELLING

Thing to Do #14

List all the superstitions you can think of, like how some buildings have no 13th floor— so the elevator goes from the 12th floor right to the 14th floor.

Did you ever wonder why a dozen is 12, not 13? Why people have 10 fingers and not 13? Why high school only goes to 12th grade? Now you know!

DING!

Hey, where's the 13th floor?

That's my stop— the ghost floor!

Time used up: Seven years of bad luck.

VISUAL DICTIONARY
OF
SUPERSTITIONS

Match the superstition with the picture: Wishing on a star, Four-leaf clover, Black cat, See a pin and pick it up and all day long you'll have good luck, Knock on wood, Step on a crack and break your mother's back, Walking under a ladder, Finding a penny, Saying "Bless you" when somebody sneezes, Horseshoe, Rabbit's foot, Break a mirror and get seven years' bad luck.

GOOD 🍀 LUCK

Thing to Do #15
   Are you lucky? Take the following quiz
to see how lucky you are.

A lucky penny gave me this idea. (I once wrote a story about a lucky penny.)

good luck—
yay!

bad luck.
oh no!

If you said yes to all 6: You are the luckiest person alive!

If you said yes to 5: You should definitely buy a lottery ticket.

If you said yes to 4: You should invest in the stock market when you grow up.

If you said yes to 3: You are one lucky dog, you!

If you said yes to 2: You are still pretty lucky.

If you said yes to 1: You need to find a four-leaf clover.

If you said yes to 0: You are beyond hope. Don't bother with a good luck charm.

Time used up: If you're lucky, all of it.

BAD LUCK

Thing to Do #16

Are you unlucky? Take the following test to see how unlucky you are.

If you said yes to 0: Buy a lottery ticket. You may be lucky!

If you said yes to 1: You need to make sure your lucky horseshoe isn't upside down by mistake.

If you said yes to 2: Don't make a bet with your friend — no way you'll win.

If you said yes to 3: Stay away from sharp objects.

If you said yes to 4: Stay inside with the drapes drawn.

If you said yes to 5: You poor devil, you.

If you said yes to 6: Get away from me — quick!

Time used up: If you're unlucky, it's already too late.

FINGER PLAY

↑ *or* If you have markers, pencils with you, you can always color your fingernails.

Thing to Do #17

   Pretend your hand is an animal. Walk it around the room. Give it a name, like Pinky or Finger Frances. Now make both your hands into animals and let them play together. They can climb furniture, race each other, dance, tickle, or argue.

Time used up: This can go on for a long while if you have a lot of imagination, and your finger pets have a lot to say.

That kid who always waves his hands around a lot, Eli— I saw him doing this at recess. It was hilarious!

I just adore your new nail polish.

Isn't it divine? The best marker available, you know.

You can draw faces on if you like.

Thing to Do #18
   If there's a lamp or strong enough
sunlight, make shadow puppets. Try
to think of new ways to use your hands,
new kinds of shapes you can make.

practice rabbit
ears or play little
Bunny Foo Foo

make a beaky
dragon

make a cup
shadow and
drink out of it

Or use your whole body and make strange
creatures.

a rare
two-legged
elephant

Time used up: In the snap of a finger.

FACE FUN

Thing to Do #19

Draw freckles on your face with marker. (Make sure it's the washable kind!) Now connect the dots. See any constellations on your cheeks? If you already have freckles, don't bother to draw new ones, just connect the ones you have.

Time used up: Depending on how freckly you are and how complicated you make your constellations, a good spot of time.

WRONG!
↓

permanent marker
↙

RIGHT!
↙

washable marker →

This kid at school named Max gave me this idea because he has lots of freckles.

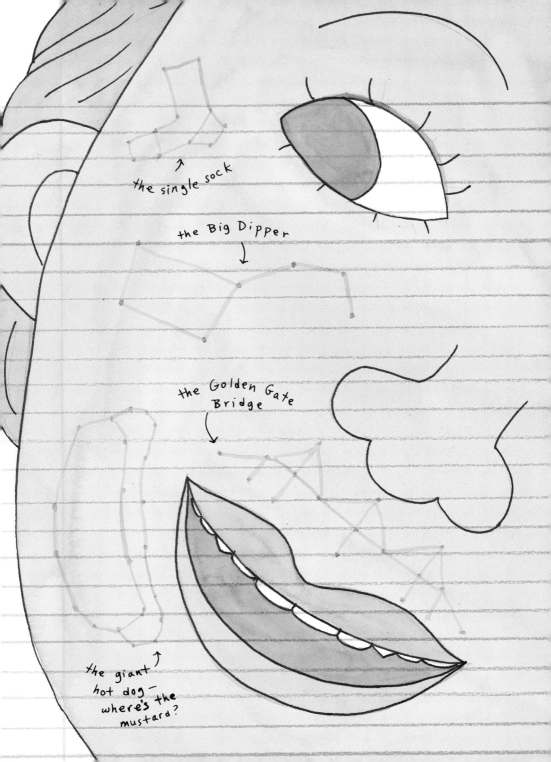

the single sock

the Big Dipper

the Golden Gate Bridge

the giant hot dog — where's the mustard?

KNOW YOURSELF

Thing to Do #20

How well do you know yourself? Take this quiz and find out! (No fair checking before you answer.)

Count the number of correct answers.

If you answered all 6 correctly: Congratulations! You are an expert on yourself.

If you answered 5 correctly: Very good — not even your mother knows you _this_ well.

If you answered 4 correctly: Not bad, but you'd better spend more time with yourself.

If you answered 3 correctly: Open your eyes! Pay attention to yourself!

If you answered 2 correctly: Careful — do you want to be a stranger to yourself?

If you answered 1 correctly: You _are_ a stranger to yourself!

If you answered 0 correctly: Better introduce yourself to yourself!

Time used up: You have your whole life to figure yourself out.

Cleo's best friend, Gigi, is always reading self-help books, but Cleo's the one who _needs_ them.

Are You a Secret Snorer? by D. Nose

self-help guides

How to Find the Real You! (Look in the yellow pages) by Hyde N. Seek

WORD GAMES

Thing to Do #21

Make up your own alphabet. Make letters that look different and have different names than plain old ABC's.

And I d
mean c
words
(what
an a

the letter
tzeek

Repeat afte
me, class.

the letter
goomph

the letter mitta
Oops! This is
just an
electrical
outlet!

Time used up: Depends on how many letters your alphabet has.

Thing to Do #22

Make up brand-new words of your own to replace ordinary, already-used words, like "bummitchel" for "bored." Then when the doctor asks, "How are you today?" you say, "I'm bummitchel!"

My carnoople is especially blatcha today.

Translation: My sister is especially grouchy today.

Like my teacher, Ms. Busby, says, "You can't flamdoodle me!"

Time used up: About snargle minutes.

Thing to Do #23

Say a word over and over again until it doesn't sound like it means anything anymore. It's just a noise.

Nose. Nose. Nose. Nose. Nose. Nose. Nose. Nose. Nose. Nose. Nose. Nose. Nose. Nose. Nose. Nose.

Time used up: Time. Time. Time. Time. Time. Time. What does "time" mean again?

The Gradual Deterioration of a Nose

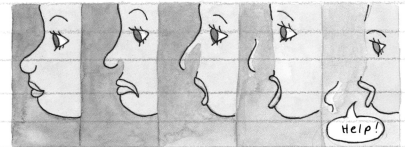

Help!

A Nose Becomes a Noise

It's too loud!

I have to give my old teacher, Mr. Nudel, credit for this one. His name made me think of it. Nudel. Noodle. Nudel. Noodel. Nudle. Noodel. Nudell. Noodell.

RHYME TIME

Thing to Do #24
Think of new, funny ways to end this rhyme:

"Roses are red,
Violets are blue..."

animal endings
(tails to you)

Possible Endings:

"Sugar is sticky
And so are you!"

match the ending
to the
beginning

"Sheep go baa
And Cows go moo."

"Almonds are nuts
And so are you."

Where is it?

"I call it a bathroom,
You call it a loo."

I feel so naked without my tail!

mad →

I don't mean that kind of expression!

EXPRESSIONS

scared ↑

This is like Mrs. Kravitz, the music teacher. She says oddball expressions all the time, like "It's no use crying over spilled lemonade."

Thing to Do #25

Think up all the figures of speech you can, like, for example:

"making a monkey out of me"

"using elbow grease"

"walking on eggshells"

"putting your nose to the grindstone"

"walking on air"

"mad as a wet hen"

"happy as a lark"

"between a rock and a hard place"

Draw pictures of what these expressions make you think of — this is the fun part!

Time used up: There's no time like the present.

Now!

Thing to Do #26

If you were good at Thing to Do #25, you'll be great at this! Think up all the expressions you can that have to do with your body.

For example:

"batting your eyelashes"

"a stomach tied in knots"

"eyes in the back of your head"

"making your skin crawl"

"cutting off your nose to spite your face"

"a broken heart"

Try drawing pictures of these. It should be pretty interesting.

Time used up: Time to wake up and smell the coffee.

Ms. Jenko, the P.E. teacher, uses these kinds of expressions, like "Put your heart into it," or "It's mind over matter." When she wants us to listen, she says, "Now kids, I want you to be all ears." I can't help thinking of Mr. Potato Head with ears in all the holes.

TWEEET

Mr. Potato "All Ears" Head

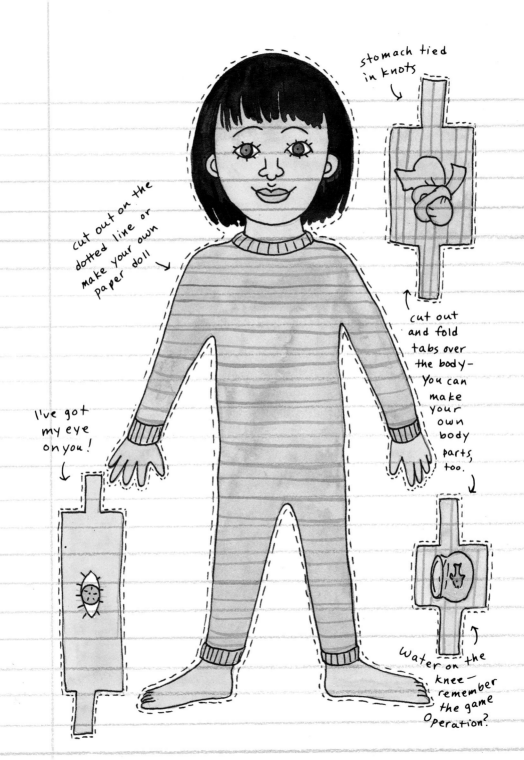

Make Your Own Fortune

Thing to Do #27
   Here's a chance to invent your <u>own</u>
expressions. Make up sayings to go
into fortune cookies.

Good things happen to those who write their own fortunes.

A cookie in need is a cookie indeed.

Those who eat fortune cookies make crumbs.

A fortune awaits you (in a cookie!).

Cleo believes in all kinds of fortune-telling, from Tarot cards to Ouija boards.

I see... orange Pekoe!

Time used up: As long as it takes for the
cookie to crumble.

crumbs — yum!
↓

Cleo reading tea leaves

Important Somebody

Thing to Do #28
   Design your own business cards.
Make them for your family and friends,

My card!

Amelia
notebook writer
   extraordinaire
(and pretty good artist)

Mrs. Kravitz
Music Teacher

"Always keeping the
   beat."

Jelly Roll Nose
CLEO
Professional Pain-
in-the-You-Know-
Where
12 years' experience

MOM
chauffeur · cook · cleaner ·
shopper · bookkeeper ·
homework helper · errand
runner · secretary · laundress ·
gardener · letter writer · etc.

SINGSONG

Carly is the jump rope expert, especially in Double Dutch.

Thing to Do #29

Make up your own jump rope songs. Use tunes you know, or make up the tune, too.

Down by the tetherball,
Down by Room One,
Johnny traded peanut
   butter
For an old bun.
He opened wide
To take a bite.
How many molars did
   Johnny lose?
One, two, three...

Porcupine, Porcupine,
Your sock has a hole.
Porcupine, Porcupine,
Stick out your toe.
Porcupine, Porcupine,
Those quills are like spikes!
Porcupine, Porcupine,
Yikes, yikes, yikes!

Time used up: Not last
night, but the night before.

Maya is good, too.

WORLD GAMES

Thing to Do #30

Make a map of the world. If you're not sure what country is where, make up your own.

Gigi can tell you the capital of any country. She's amazing. She even knows the names of countries that don't exist. (When she's mad at Cleo, she says Cleo belongs in the Land of the Nanny-Nanny-Hoo-Hoos.)

REALLY FREEZING-LAND

SWEDEN

NORWAY

FINLAND

OVER THE RAINBOW-LAND

BRRR COLD-LAND

WHALE ISLAND

OINK-LAND

LA DI DA-LAND

GERMANY

ROCK LAND

YOU'RE LOST-LAND

ARE WE THERE YET?-LAND

FRANCE

JELLY BEAN-LAND

YADA YADA-LAND

GRAY GREY-LAND

SPAIN

ITALY

THERE-LAND

SOMEWHERE LAND

HERE I AM-LAND

THERE'S NO THERE-LAND

TIC-TAC-TOE-LAND

LAND-LAND

Time used up: Pacific standard time, Greenwich mean time, daylight saving time.

wiener dog flag ↗

Thing to Do #31

Design flags to go with your countries, or make new flags to replace the ones countries already have.

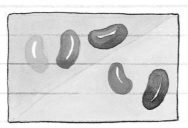

JELLY BEAN-LAND

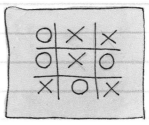

TIC-TAC-TOE-LAND

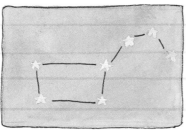

OVER THE RAINBOW-LAND

REALLY FREEZING-LAND

Time used up: International time.

Thing to Do #32

Design your own postage stamp collection. What or who would you like to see commemorated on a stamp?

Draw your own!

birthday cakes of the rich and famous ↘

Mako, my Japanese pen pal, sent me some great stamps on his letters, so I thought I'd make my own.

favorite teddy bears ↗

↙ snazzy swimming pools

designer socks ↑

Time used up: You know how slow the post office is!

Great Vegetables I Have Known
(but not necessarily eaten)

IT'S GOOD
₄ FOR YOU ₄

CORN ON THE COB
10¢   mmm!

TOE-MAY-TOE
3¢

33¢
TOE-MAH-TOE

20¢
PEA·PEA·PEA

18¢
Have you ever seen a carrot wear glasses?

Grown-ups Famous for Distinguishing Features

31¢
AUNT BEA—
BAD BREATH!

THE LARGE MOLE
SUBSTITUTE TEACHER
12¢

SHARP NAILS
CAFETERIA LADY   7¢

THE DENTIST
16¢
HAIRY NOSTRILS

Dogs of the Neighborhood

SPARKY
15¢

BUTCH
6¢

10¢ Sausage 10¢

DOG WITH EAR MUFFINS
LULU 5¢

FOOD FOR THOUGHT

Thing to Do #33:
 Make a list of good foods and gross foods. Post it on the refrigerator when you're finished so your mom or dad will know what to make for dinner.

YES! MAKE IT! GOOD!	NO! Forget About It! BAD!
pizza	liver
spaghetti	green beans
french fries	peas
baked potato	brussels sprouts
grilled cheese	anchovies
corn on the cob	sardines
biscuits	any fish
mashed potato	any pudding with funny
pie	little bumps in it, like
ice cream	tapioca (tapiyuccha)—
muffins	don't even try it!
cookies	onions
cupcakes	anything that's runny
	and gooey-looking
	like raw egg —
	yucch!

Time used up: Enough time to make a tasty batch of cookies.

There's this kid at school, Melissa, who says there are no nasty foods, but then, she'll eat any thing. She loves cafeteria food, even Mystery Mush.

Mystery Mush — part stew, part dog food

Thing to Do #34

Using foods only from your good list (of course), draw a menu of your idea of the PERFECT meal. Use this as a hint for the cook in your house.

Le Café Chez Me!

~appetizer~
cheesy crackers (no stinky cheeses — first choice is the kind that comes out of a can)

~salad~

Jell-O with marshmallows (yes, this counts as a green salad if it's lime Jell-O)

↑ wiggling the Jell-O is permitted

~main~
dish
pizza, spaghetti, or
fried chicken
(french fries are optional)

↑ all can be eaten with fingers — even the spaghetti!

~dessert~
ice cream sundae with fudge sauce, whipped cream, and a maraschino cherry

← Six flavors is just fine!

Time used up: Dinner time!

SCIENTIFIC EXPERIMENTS
without test tubes!

Thing to Do #35

Pretend your room is a paleological dig and you are excavating for fossils. Carefully label your finds. (This will work in the car, too.)

This one is in honor of my mom, who is always threatening to carbon-date the socks under my bed.

protective cotton
↓

Petrified Pretzel

Fossilized Cheerio

Prehistoric Puzzle Piece

tissue
↓

Bug Preserved in Amber of Ancient Lollipop

Is your room clean?

Lump of Dried-Out Play-Doh Pressed Flat in Sedimentary Layers of Sheets and Blankets

Time used up: Eons and eons.

Thing to Do #36

Pretend you are an alien from another planet. Try to describe your surroundings and what earthlings are like to your fellow aliens.

Time used up: Light years.

SCIENCE IN ACTION

Thing to Do #37
  Design useful inventions, like an automatic clothes-folder or a pill you can chew instead of brushing your teeth.

Nadia is always thinking of ways to get out of doing work, like the old shove-everything-under-your-bed-to-clean-your-room gambit.

Cleo Alarm

INTRUDER ALERT

clip onto your pocket, light flashes yellow when Cleo enters range — when she is really near, light turns red and beeping sound warns you — BEWARE!

Miracle Food Additive

YUCCH TO YUM TASTE TRANSFORMER

One drop of this amazing formula turns any gross food into a good food. Presto-chango! Broccoli becomes brownies, liver becomes lasagna, and mushrooms become maraschino cherries.

I'm done, Mom.

De-Raisiner

Is your oatmeal ruined by wrinkly raisins? Do you want to remove unsightly dried fruit from your cookies? Then this is the invention for you!

Is your mom mad at you? Are you about to be sent to your room? Never fear! Mood Softener is here! Spray gently in front of the angry parent and within seconds, you'll be offered a special treat!

Go to your room, young lady!

Want to get some ice cream?

Mood Softener

before →

← after

creative time-keeping

Time used up: Invent a new kind of clock! Make your own time system — why be stuck with hours and minutes when you can have churkas and loomies?

P E N C I L   P O W E R

Thing to Do #38
 Think of great first sentences for a
story. Then think of the rest of the story.

① "Oh, no!" Jones shouted as she stepped
    into the room.

② The drums were beating steadily, a
    bad sign for sure.

③ There was no question that this was the
    largest bug Alfred had ever seen.

④ It's not easy to stuff a suitcase with 62
    jars of cranberry jelly, but that's just
    what Shirley did.

⑤ The clouds boiled in the pot of sky.

Time used up: Once upon a time.

Leah and I took turns writing a story this way. It was a lot of fun.
And we ended up with a pretty good tale.

Thing to Do #39

Do the same thing for cartoons. Draw several first panels for a comic strip. Then go back and draw what comes next.

Time used up: Later that day...

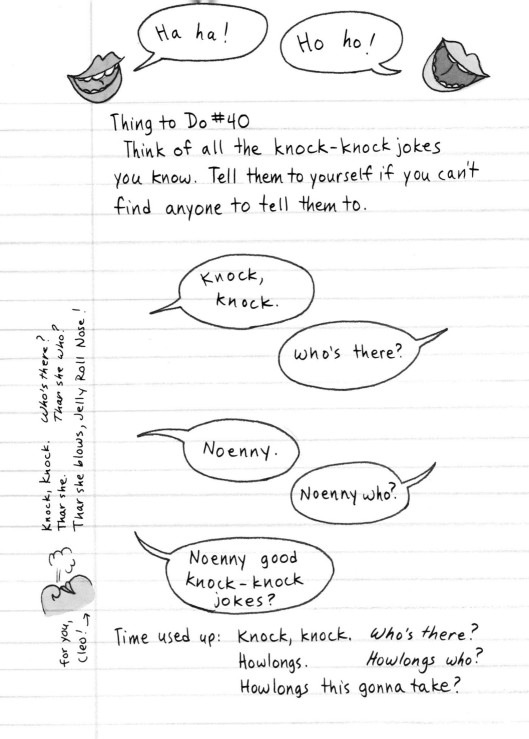

Thing to Do #40
  Think of all the knock-knock jokes
you know. Tell them to yourself if you can't
find anyone to tell them to.

What's an undercover store?

Where you buy a bed!

Thing to Do #41

Have some pun! Get it? That's a pun — pun, fun — get it? Okay, you got it. Now make up some puns of your own. Draw pictures to go with them.

Ms. Busby is the Queen of Puns. She doesn't tell a lot of jokes, but she loves puns.

Bald man's motto: "Hair today, gone tomorrow."

DANGER: RADIATION

Gone fission

Sign on atomic scientist's door

Did you hear about the eager potato?

It's all eyes!

What does the butcher say to her customers? "Pleased to meat you!"

Time used up: What time did the kid go to the dentist? Two-thirty. (Tooth-hurty!)

Thing to Do #42

Now that you're in a punny mood, make up cute business names, ones that are puns or jokes, like a pet store called "The Doggy in the Window" or a hair salon called "Shear Delight."

Bakery called "You Take the Cake"

Indian café called "Delhi Deli"

Pizza place called "Pie in the Sky"

SIZE 10 AAA

Is this a shoe size or a battery?

Shoe store called "If the Shoe Fits, Wear It"

Did you hear about the electronics store?

It's called "Batteries Included!"

Time used up: A portable-clock store called "Tick Tock Tote."

Name That Face!

Thing to Do #43:

Give a new name to everyone in your family. Then try to find the perfect name for your friends. Think of names that <u>really</u> fit their personalities. (Some people might <u>already</u> have names that are exactly like who they are — like me, Amelia!)

I'm waaaa-aaaiting!

Cleo really acts and looks like a Bertha — she even <u>sounds</u> like a Bertha (especially when she burps!).

Mom's real name is Patience — something she definitely does not have a lot of. Her name should be Enid or Roxanne.

Time used up: A minute by any other name would last as long.

Carly wants to change her name to Zeena, but if she can't do that, she'll settle for Carlotta. She says she just doesn't feel like a Carly.

House of Cards

← careful! Don't shake them!

Thing to Do #44
  Design your own deck of cards. Then play War with yourself. Or 52-Card Pickup. Make up your own card game and give it a great name, like Lucky Fours, Doodle, or Thumbkin.

WAR!   WAR!

Time used up: Time for Crazy Eights, Spit, Hearts, Casino, Gin Rummy, Fish, Seven Card Stud, Five Card Draw, Twenty-One, Honeymoon Bridge, Canasta, Solitaire, Old Maid, Pinochle, Idiot, and WAR!

veeery interesting!

I get all the credit for this idea myself. I'm the Queen ♥ of Good Ideas.

3 of Cupcakes

4 of Cheese

9 of Yo Yos

Deuce of Toothbrushes

Ace of Peanut Butter

8 of Eyeglasses

Queen of Dalmatians

10 of Socks

6 of Lemons

7 of Crayons

Jack of Dragons

5 of Ice Cream Cones

Thing to Do #45
  Make certificates for your family and friends.
Think about what each person does especially
well.

This Award Certifies That

Leah

is the best, neatest underwear
folder in the world

For Faithful and Frequent
Letter Writing
the highly coveted
Blue Ribbon Stamp
Award
to
Nadia

Nadia got an award for best story at the Young Authors Fair, but I've never gotten an award for anything!

GOLD AWARD
for
Elegant

Table Manners
(<u>never</u> chews with her mouth open!)

Gigi

The Silver Q Award

Q

is for
Queasy
and the
Queen of
Queasiness,
Her Majesty,
~ Cleo ~

← air sickness bag

← car sickness bag

The
Double Jump-Rope
Certificate
Best Double Dutch Rope Jumper
Carly

Time used up: Time to present an award!
(Think up a good toast to go with it.)

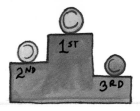

Thing to Do #46
   OK, you've designed business cards, menus, and award certificates — now here's your chance to design your own OLYMPICS! What events would you include? Now try training for each event. (And think of the snazzy athletic wear to go with each sport.)

   For example:

Popcorn Toss
   The athlete needs nerves of steel and keen concentration. A second of inattention means the popcorn hits the
      floor — or worse yet,
      your forehead —
      instead of your mouth.

Gold Medal for Popcorn Toss

Judges consider the height of the popcorn's flight when giving out the scores.

Chair - Spinning

A sense of balance, keen reflexes, and most important, a stomach that isn't easily queasy are essential in this sport. The athlete must spin as long as possible without getting miserably dizzy. The faster the spin, the higher the score.

after a successful spin

note the fashionable spin-suit

Floor - Sliding

A good, slippery waxed floor and some socks are all the equipment necessary. The length of the slide matters most, but style and speed also count.

setting a record!

Time used up: Every four years.

Thing to Do # 47
  Now it's time for some mental Olympics with the Total Trivia Quiz. See how well you do.

This is a companion to the Know Yourself Quiz — how well do you know everything else?

① How many tines does the average fork have?

② Does your toilet flush clockwise or counter-clockwise?

I just hope it flushes!

③ How many sips does it take to drink a cup of hot cocoa?

④ Does soda have any nutritional value?

Does sugar count?

⑤ How long does a balloon last if no one pops it?

Do these things ever die?

⑥ What are those orange candy peanuts actually made of?

It's a mystery!

If you got 0 right : You're just an average
   person with no interest in the details around you.
If you got 1 right: You are not very observant.
  Better check to see if your fly is zipped.
If you got 2 right: Not bad — maybe you just
  need to open your eyes wider.
If you got 3 right: You are sensitive to the
  finer things in life.
If you got 4 right: You are very perceptive
  and have a sharp mind.
If you got 5 right: You can easily earn a
   Ph.D. in Trivia — congratulations!
If you got 6 right: You're a genius! Can I
   have your autograph?
If you got 7 right: Hey, you cheated!
 · (Or you didn't even notice how many
   questions there are.)

  Time used up! Time to pay attention!
sharp eyes noticing everything! ➘

MORE MAPS

Thing to Do #48
 Draw a diagram of your brain. Label all the
relevant parts.

Thing to Do #49
 Make a map of your heart. Label each section.
Time used up: In a heartbeat!

See, Mr. Nadel, I'm using my noodle!

What about rhymes, puns, useful information?

writing
and
drawing

books
and
comics

noticing
noses

games and
puzzles

imagination

playing
with
numbers

computer

not-so-
great
ideas

t.v.

great
ideas

think about all the things you love — maybe too many to fit!

inventions,
cool science
stuff

family
(OK, Cleo, this
includes you)

books,
stories,
pictures

friends

beautiful
places like
Yosemite

my
room

chocolate

starry
skies

Thing to Do #50
  You know those notebooks with the Tables of
Useful Information on the back cover? Here's
your chance to make your own Useful Information
Page. Think of all those things you <u>really</u> want
to know.

Table of Mom Minutes

"In a minute" when she's cooking = 20 minutes
"In a minute" when she's reading = 15 minutes
"In a minute" when she's in the shower = 30 minutes
"In a minute" when she's on the phone = 2 hours

Measure of Doctor's Idea of Pain

"This won't hurt a bit." = it will hurt a little
"Now, this is just going to sting." = it will hurt a lot
"It will all be over in a second." = YEOUCH!

GROWN-UPS:
WHAT THEY
   SAY
   AND
WHAT THEY
   MEAN

Time used up: A mom minute. (Yes, but which
one?)

I can't believe it — just as I finish this guide, before I have a chance to actually USE it, here comes Cleo. Wouldn't you know it! Now we have to go, and I can't do any of the cool things I wrote down.

Oh well, maybe I'll get lucky and there'll be a big traffic jam. I'll be ready!